THE

BIOGRAPHY

OF

REUBEN OWEN

BY

Ronald S. Isaacs

All rights reserved © 2024

The scanning, uploading, and disseminating of this work online or by any other means without the author's written consent is prohibited and unlawful, unless allowed by the U.S. Copyright Act of 1976. Please do not engage in or promote the electronic piracy of protected content; instead, only buy authorized paperback and electronic versions. The purpose of this publication is to offer knowledgeable and trustworthy information on the topics discussed

Table of Contents

CHAPTER 1 1

  Introduction 1

  Purpose of the Biography 1

  Overview of Reuben Owen's Life 3

CHAPTER 2 6

  Early Life and Background 6

  Birth and Family History 6

  Childhood and Education 8

  Early Influences 11

CHAPTER 3 16

  Career Beginnings 16

  First Steps into Work Life 16

  Challenges and Early Achievements 19

CHAPTER 4 25

  Rise to Prominence 25

  Breakthrough Moments 25

  Key Projects and Accomplishments 29

  Public Recognition 34

CHAPTER 5 38

    Personal Life 38

        Family and Relationships 38

        Hobbies and Interests 42

        Personal Values and Beliefs 46

CHAPTER 6 50

    Impact and Legacy 50

        Contributions to Society or Industry 50

        Influence on Others 54

        Awards and Honors 58

CHAPTER 7 61

    Challenges and Controversies 61

        Public Criticisms 61

        How He Overcame Obstacles 64

CHAPTER 8 69

Current Life and Future Plans 69

        Recent Activities 69

        Vision for the Future 71

        Conclusion 75

Summary of Key Points 75

Final Thoughts on Reuben Owen's Life 77

CHAPTER 1

Introduction

Purpose of the Biography

The purpose of this biography is to present a comprehensive and insightful account of the life, experiences, and contributions of Reuben Owen, a figure whose journey offers valuable lessons and inspiration. This biography seeks to go beyond the surface details of dates and events, delving into the motivations, values, challenges, and triumphs that have shaped Reuben Owen into the person he is known as today.

Reuben Owen's story is one marked by determination, resilience, and a commitment to excellence whether in his professional endeavors, personal life, or community engagements. By documenting his early beginnings, the influences that shaped his character, and the milestones he has achieved, this biography aims to provide a holistic understanding of his life's journey.

This work is intended for a diverse audience: those who admire Reuben Owen's accomplishments, researchers seeking insight into his industry or field, students looking for role models, and anyone interested in real-life narratives of growth, leadership, and perseverance. It offers an opportunity to explore how personal choices, opportunities, and responses to adversity can define a person's legacy.

Furthermore, this biography serves as a historical and motivational document. It preserves the memory of Reuben Owen's journey for future generations and highlights the values of hard work, integrity, and innovation. It also underscores the importance of personal development and community impact, encouraging readers to reflect on their own paths and aspirations.

Ultimately, this biography aims not only to tell the story of Reuben Owen but also to celebrate the human spirit, inspire excellence, and remind readers that greatness often emerges from humble beginnings and is forged through dedication, vision, and a strong sense of purpose.

Overview of Reuben Owen's Life

Reuben Owen is a British farmer, television personality, and public figure known for his deep connection to rural life and his appearance in the popular television series Our Yorkshire Farm and its follow-up, Beyond the Yorkshire Farm. From a young age, Reuben demonstrated a strong work ethic, a natural affinity for the land, and a practical skillset that set him apart from his peers. As the eldest son of Clive and Amanda Owen, who rose to fame for their traditional farming lifestyle in the Yorkshire Dales, Reuben quickly became a familiar face to viewers across the UK

Born into a large family of nine children, Reuben's upbringing was anything but ordinary. Life on Ravenseat Farm taught him the importance of hard work, teamwork, and resilience in the face of nature's unpredictability. From an early age, he took part in the daily routines of the farm tending to animals, repairing machinery, and navigating the rugged landscape of North Yorkshire. His exposure to the farming lifestyle helped him develop practical skills that would later form the foundation of his career.

As he grew older, Reuben began to carve out his own identity and ambitions. With a growing interest in mechanical work, he pursued a path in heavy machinery and construction, eventually starting his own business. This move marked the beginning of his transition from a young farm boy to an independent entrepreneur, a journey that was documented in the Beyond the Yorkshire Farm series. The show not only highlighted his technical capabilities but also emphasized his leadership qualities and determination to succeed on his own terms.

Despite the public attention, Reuben remains grounded and closely tied to his rural roots. He continues to inspire many with his practical knowledge, down-to-earth demeanor, and commitment to building a meaningful life through honest work. Whether on-screen or behind the scenes, Reuben Owen's life is a testament to the enduring values of family, hard work, and perseverance in an ever-changing world.

This biography offers an in-depth look into Reuben's life, from his early days on Ravenseat Farm to his current role as a young leader forging his path in the farming and construction industries. It celebrates the growth of a boy shaped by the land into a young man whose journey resonates with audiences across generations.

CHAPTER 2

Early Life and Background

Birth and Family History

Reuben Owen was born in 2003 in the rugged and picturesque region of the Yorkshire Dales, England. He is the eldest son of Clive Owen and Amanda Owen, who gained national recognition as the stars of the Channel 5 documentary series Our Yorkshire Farm. The series followed their lives as traditional hill shepherds on Ravenseat Farm, a remote, 2,000-acre working farm nestled in Swaledale, one of the most remote parts of Northern England.

Reuben is one of nine children in the Owen family, who became known to millions for their self-sufficient lifestyle, strong family values, and commitment to preserving a way of life that is rapidly vanishing in modern Britain. Growing up in a large, close-knit family meant that Reuben was never short of company, and each sibling played a role in the everyday workings of the farm. From a young age, Reuben was expected to take on responsibilities and contribute to the demanding routines of rural life.

His mother, Amanda Owen, also known as the "Yorkshire Shepherdess," is a bestselling author and public speaker who has documented her life on the farm through books and media appearances. His father, Clive Owen, is a practical, experienced shepherd who has spent decades farming in the Dales. Together, they raised their children to value hard work, independence, and resilience qualities that would deeply influence Reuben's own character and future ambitions.

The Owen family's lifestyle stood in stark contrast to that of many modern households. With limited access to urban conveniences, the family relied on their own labor, cooperation, and deep knowledge of the land. Daily chores, including tending to sheep, fixing machinery, and helping with construction work, were part of Reuben's early life, shaping his strong sense of responsibility and practical skillset.

Reuben's upbringing in this unique environment was not just a testament to traditional farming life it was also a story of love, determination, and unity. The bond within the Owen family, forged through shared hardship and collective effort, became a core aspect of their identity and a compelling feature of the television series that brought their story to the public.

This strong foundation in family and rural life would later guide Reuben as he ventured out into the world, determined to build his own legacy while remaining rooted in the values instilled in him from birth.

Childhood and Education

Reuben Owen's childhood was shaped by the rugged beauty and demanding lifestyle of Ravenseat Farm, situated deep within the Yorkshire Dales. Raised in a family that prioritized hands-on experience over luxury, Reuben's early years were far removed from the typical modern upbringing. With no nearby neighbors, limited internet access, and a daily routine dictated by the land and livestock, his childhood was deeply rooted in nature, hard work, and self-reliance.

From as young as six years old, Reuben became actively involved in the day-to-day operations of the family farm. His chores included feeding animals, helping with sheep herding, repairing fences, and operating farm machinery under supervision. Unlike many children who spend their early years indoors or behind screens, Reuben spent most of his time outdoors, learning the rhythms of farming life and developing practical skills that would later become central to his career.

Education for Reuben followed a non-traditional path. He attended a local school in the Dales, but his most formative education arguably took place at home and on the farm. His parents, especially his mother Amanda Owen, believed strongly in the value of giving their children the freedom to explore, learn through doing, and develop independence. This philosophy allowed Reuben to blend academic learning with real-world experience an education grounded in both books and the soil beneath his feet.

Although he was not known to excel academically in the conventional sense, Reuben showed an early aptitude for mechanical work, construction, and problem-solving skills that often cannot be measured by classroom tests but are essential in practical environments. He displayed a keen interest in machinery, often helping his father with tractors and tools, and quickly became known for his mechanical know-how within the family and local community.

As he progressed into his teenage years, Reuben began to consider how to apply his interests and talents beyond the farm. While still helping his parents, he started taking on external jobs in construction and groundwork, gaining valuable experience and gradually transitioning into professional work. This balance between formal schooling, hands-on learning, and early entrepreneurship played a critical role in shaping his identity as a skilled young man with ambition and direction.

Reuben's educational journey, though unconventional, exemplifies the strength of learning rooted in experience, curiosity, and purpose. It laid the foundation for his eventual move into business, showing that education does not only happen in classrooms it thrives wherever there is a willingness to learn and grow.

Early Influences

Reuben Owen's early life was rich with influences that helped shape his character, work ethic, and career path. Growing up on Ravenseat Farm, nestled in the remote and scenic Yorkshire Dales, Reuben was immersed from birth in a world where nature, manual labor, and self-reliance were daily realities. The most powerful and consistent influences in his early years came from his family, environment, and exposure to practical work from a very young age.

Family Influence

The foundation of Reuben's values and worldview was undoubtedly laid by his parents, Clive and Amanda Owen. As traditional hill shepherds, they lived a lifestyle that required physical toughness, resourcefulness, and unwavering commitment. From his father, Reuben learned the importance of discipline, reliability, and hands-on problem-solving skills crucial in farming and beyond. His father's quiet strength and steady approach to challenges left a lasting mark on Reuben's personality.

His mother, Amanda, played an equally vital role in nurturing his independence and curiosity. Known as the "Yorkshire Shepherdess," Amanda encouraged her children to explore their interests and to take initiative, even at an early age. Her storytelling through books and media appearances also showed Reuben how one's life and work could resonate with a wider audience perhaps planting the seed for his later involvement in television.

Life on the Farm

The physical environment of the Yorkshire Dales with its vast, open landscapes, unpredictable weather, and tough terrain was itself a silent but powerful teacher. Living and working in such conditions instilled in Reuben a sense of resilience and adaptability. There was no luxury of ease or idleness; every day required effort, and every task had meaning. This early exposure to hard, honest labor fostered a maturity and practical mindset far beyond his years.

Mechanical and Practical Work

Another major influence in Reuben's life was his growing interest in machinery and construction. From a young age, he was drawn to tractors, diggers, and farm equipment. He enjoyed learning how things worked, how to fix them, and eventually how to operate heavy machinery himself. His passion for mechanics and building things was supported by his parents, who encouraged his independence and trusted him with responsibilities most children his age wouldn't encounter.

As he began assisting with more complex projects such as land clearing, vehicle maintenance, and groundwork Reuben discovered a path that aligned naturally with his interests. These experiences planted the seeds for his eventual career in construction and groundwork, and he began taking small external jobs while still in his teens.

Media Exposure

Although not a conventional influence, Reuben's exposure to public life through the television series Our Yorkshire Farm also played a significant role in shaping his confidence and communication skills. Appearing on national television from a young age, he developed a strong sense of self-awareness and the ability to articulate his experiences a quality that would later help him as he stepped into his own spotlight in Beyond the Yorkshire Farm.

Reuben Owen's early influences were a blend of family, environment, and hands-on experience. These forces combined to shape a young man who is practical, grounded, hardworking, and increasingly independent traits that continue to define his journey as he builds a future on his own terms.

CHAPTER 3

Career Beginnings

First Steps into Work Life

Reuben Owen's entry into the world of work came naturally and progressively, molded by the unique environment of his upbringing and the early responsibilities he took on at Ravenseat Farm. Long before reaching adulthood, Reuben had already developed the mindset and skillset of a working man, thanks to years of contributing to his family's demanding agricultural lifestyle.

From his pre-teen years, Reuben was actively involved in the day-to-day running of the farm. His earliest work experiences were not formal jobs, but rather the routine, essential tasks that made up farm life herding sheep, mending fences, handling tools, operating basic machinery, and assisting in seasonal tasks like shearing or lambing. These responsibilities were part of everyday life, and they played a critical role in building Reuben's confidence, physical ability, and work ethic.

However, as he grew older, Reuben began to gravitate toward mechanical and construction-related tasks. He demonstrated an exceptional interest in machinery particularly tractors, diggers, and various forms of agricultural equipment. Fascinated by how things worked, he not only learned to operate machinery but also began troubleshooting and repairing them, often taking initiative beyond what was expected of someone his age.

By his mid-teens, Reuben had started taking on small jobs outside the family farm. He began helping neighbors and local farmers with groundwork, fencing, and equipment handling. His reputation for being reliable, capable, and hardworking quickly spread in the local area, leading to more requests for his assistance. This period marked a key transition Reuben was no longer just helping on the family farm; he was earning money and building a name for himself as a young tradesman.

Driven by a desire for independence and fueled by his passion for machinery, Reuben took the bold step of venturing into self-employment. He began acquiring tools, working part-time alongside his father, and eventually investing in his own machinery to launch a small-scale groundworks and digger operation. This decision marked the official beginning of his professional work life and set the stage for his growing success.

This early phase of Reuben's work life was also captured in the television series Beyond the Yorkshire Farm, which documented his journey into business with the support of his father Clive. The program offered viewers a glimpse into the practical challenges he faced managing projects, handling equipment, balancing budgets, and learning leadership on the job. The show highlighted not only his technical abilities but also his ambition, determination, and problem-solving skills.

Reuben's first steps into the world of work reflect the values instilled in him from childhood: self-sufficiency, honesty, and perseverance. Unlike many who ease into employment through school-to-career transitions, Reuben entered the workforce through hands-on experience, community trust, and a strong desire to forge his own path.

Challenges and Early Achievements

Reuben Owen's transition from life on the family farm to launching his own business was not without its share of obstacles. Like many young people stepping into independence, Reuben faced a range of challenges that tested his patience, perseverance, and resolve. However, through these trials, he also achieved remarkable milestones that laid a strong foundation for his future.

Challenges

1. Age and Inexperience

One of the first and most significant challenges Reuben faced was his youth. Starting out in the groundwork and machinery business at a relatively young age meant that some people underestimated his ability and doubted his professionalism. Gaining the trust of clients and being taken seriously in a competitive field required maturity, clear communication, and consistent demonstration of skill.

2. Financial Constraints

Starting a business from scratch, especially in a field requiring expensive machinery and equipment, presented a major hurdle. Reuben had to be strategic with his resources, often working long hours and taking on multiple small jobs to afford basic tools and machinery. He also had to learn how to budget, price jobs fairly, and manage income responsibly skills he developed gradually through real-world experience.

3. Balancing Public Exposure and Private Growth

Being a public figure from a young age brought its own set of pressures. As someone who grew up in the spotlight thanks to Our Yorkshire Farm and later Beyond the Yorkshire Farm, Reuben had to balance the expectations of an audience with the reality of learning and making mistakes. He navigated this by staying grounded, avoiding distractions from fame, and focusing on personal and professional growth.

4. Technical and Logistical Setbacks

Every job Reuben took came with its own set of physical and logistical challenges from equipment breakdowns and bad weather to unexpected site complications. These situations tested his problem-solving abilities and required him to remain calm under pressure. Instead of being discouraged, Reuben used these setbacks as learning experiences, constantly improving his craft and expanding his skill set.

Early Achievements

Despite these challenges, Reuben accomplished a number of significant milestones in his early work life that highlighted his capability and resilience:

1. Launching His Own Business

One of Reuben's most impressive early achievements was the successful launch of his own groundworks and digger business. He did this while still in his teens, managing real jobs with real clients and operating independently in a demanding industry. This move demonstrated not only his technical expertise but also his entrepreneurial mindset.

2. Building a Client Base

Through word of mouth and his growing reputation, Reuben quickly established a small but steady network of clients who trusted him for groundwork, landscaping, and mechanical tasks. His reliability and work ethic helped build long-term working relationships, something many older professionals struggle to achieve early in their careers.

3. National Recognition Through Television

Reuben's starring role in Beyond the Yorkshire Farm not only showcased his work to a national audience but also helped promote the dignity of trades and rural entrepreneurship. The series allowed him to inspire other young people to pursue practical, hands-on careers, proving that success doesn't only come through traditional academic routes.

4. Earning Respect in the Community

In a profession that often favors experience and age, Reuben managed to earn the respect of his peers, mentors, and clients through dedication and consistency. His growing independence and professionalism were a testament to the values instilled in him from his upbringing on Ravenseat Farm.

Reuben Owen's early career journey is a powerful example of how determination, practical skill, and resilience can overcome the barriers of age, doubt, and inexperience. His ability to meet challenges head-on while achieving real progress in his chosen field marks him as an inspiring figure for young entrepreneurs and tradespeople alike.

CHAPTER 4

Rise to Prominence

Breakthrough Moments

Every career journey features defining points that shift momentum and pave the way for greater success. For Reuben Owen, several breakthrough moments marked his transition from a hardworking young farmhand to a respected entrepreneur and public figure. These moments were not only milestones in his professional journey but also reflections of his growth, passion, and dedication.

1. Launch of Beyond the Yorkshire Farm

One of Reuben's most pivotal breakthrough moments came with the debut of the television series Beyond the Yorkshire Farm in 2022. A spin-off from the highly successful Our Yorkshire Farm, this show placed Reuben at the center, documenting his efforts to launch and grow his own groundwork business.

The series offered viewers a close look at Reuben's drive, technical skills, and problem-solving abilities, as well as the unique challenges of running a small rural business. It also highlighted the strong bond between Reuben and his father, Clive, who appeared alongside him to offer support and guidance. The show was well-received and brought Reuben into the national spotlight not as a child of famous parents, but as a capable, hardworking young man carving his own path.

This exposure helped validate his journey and introduced his business and personality to a wider audience, opening doors to new clients, partnerships, and opportunities.

2. Acquisition of His First Digger

Another defining moment in Reuben's career was when he purchased his first digger with money earned from small jobs. This investment symbolized more than just ownership of a machine it marked the beginning of his independence as a tradesman. With this tool, Reuben could take on more complex projects, increase his earnings, and operate with greater flexibility.

Owning his own equipment also helped establish credibility within the local community. It showed that he was serious, self-sufficient, and capable of handling real-world work an important step for any young entrepreneur.

3. Managing Independent Projects

As Reuben began managing jobs independently planning, executing, and completing groundwork tasks for clients he proved that he could function professionally without constant supervision. These projects became key turning points that demonstrated his readiness to operate as a full-fledged contractor rather than just a helper.

Some of these early jobs, captured in Beyond the Yorkshire Farm, involved difficult terrain, tight deadlines, and logistical complications, but Reuben handled them with determination and practical wisdom beyond his years. Successfully completing these projects boosted his reputation and self-confidence.

4. Gaining Public Respect as an Independent Identity

Another breakthrough moment came as the public began to recognize Reuben not only as a member of the Owen family but as an individual with his own identity and ambitions. Through his actions, interviews, and business growth, he emerged from behind the image of "just one of the kids on the farm" to become a relatable figure for young people pursuing skilled trades.

Many admired his grounded nature, humility, and hands-on approach to life and work. This growing recognition served to strengthen his public image and allowed him to serve as a role model for those considering alternative career paths outside of traditional academic systems.

Reuben Owen's breakthrough moments reflect a journey built on initiative, courage, and consistency. Whether it was investing in his first piece of equipment, leading his own projects, or stepping into the spotlight with maturity and skill, these milestones continue to define his remarkable story and hint at even greater achievements ahead.

Key Projects and Accomplishments

Reuben Owen's early career is distinguished by a number of significant projects and achievements that showcase his technical skills, entrepreneurial spirit, and growing reputation within the rural trades community. These accomplishments have not only validated his abilities but have also helped establish his footprint in the groundwork and machinery sectors.

1. Successful Launch and Management of His Own Groundworks Business

One of Reuben's most notable accomplishments is the successful establishment of his groundworks and digger hire business. Starting with limited resources, Reuben was able to scale up by taking on varied contracts ranging from land clearing and excavation to fencing and landscaping. His business has served local farms, rural homeowners, and small construction projects, reflecting his versatility and reliability.

The ability to manage the operational, financial, and logistical aspects of the business at a young age is a testament to Reuben's maturity and dedication. This venture laid the foundation for his future ambitions in the construction and trades industry.

2. Complex Excavation and Landscaping Projects

Among the many jobs Reuben has undertaken, several stand out for their complexity and successful execution. These include hillside excavations, drainage installations, and landscaping projects on challenging terrains within the Yorkshire Dales. Such projects required not only mechanical skill but also careful planning and adaptability to changing weather and ground conditions.

His work in these projects earned him praise from clients for precision, professionalism, and respect for the environment qualities highly valued in rural contracting work.

3. Restoration and Maintenance of Farm Infrastructure

Reuben has also played a critical role in the ongoing maintenance and restoration of infrastructure on Ravenseat Farm itself. Tasks such as repairing stone walls, installing new fencing, and maintaining farm tracks have been essential to the farm's operation and longevity. His contributions here demonstrate a strong connection to his roots and an understanding of traditional farming needs.

These efforts were frequently featured on television, helping to highlight the importance of preserving rural heritage while embracing modern techniques.

4. Television Appearances and Public Recognition

Through Beyond the Yorkshire Farm, Reuben has gained national recognition, not just as a family member but as a skilled tradesman in his own right. The show has documented many of his key projects, giving the public an insight into the hard work and expertise involved in groundwork and machinery operation.

His media presence has broadened his influence, inspiring young viewers and helping to break down stereotypes about rural trades and entrepreneurship.

5. Building a Positive Reputation in the Local Community

Perhaps one of Reuben's most valuable accomplishments is the reputation he has built within the local community. Known for his reliability, honesty, and willingness to take on challenging jobs, he has earned the trust of clients and peers alike.

This goodwill has translated into repeat business and word-of-mouth referrals, essential components for long-term success in rural trades.

Reuben Owen's key projects and accomplishments reflect a young man who has combined practical skills with entrepreneurial savvy to create a promising career. From managing complex groundwork tasks to gaining public recognition, Reuben continues to build a legacy rooted in hard work, integrity, and passion for his craft.

Public Recognition

Reuben Owen's journey from a farmhand in the Yorkshire Dales to a recognized public figure is a testament to his hard work, authenticity, and the unique platform provided by television. His public recognition extends beyond his family's fame, highlighting his individual achievements and growing influence as a young entrepreneur and tradesman.

1. Television Exposure and Media Presence

Reuben first appeared on screens as part of the popular documentary series Our Yorkshire Farm, which showcased the lives of the Owen family. However, it was with the launch of Beyond the Yorkshire Farm that Reuben truly stepped into the spotlight as the central figure. The show focused on his efforts to establish his own groundwork and machinery business, providing viewers with an intimate look at the challenges and rewards of rural entrepreneurship.

This exposure introduced Reuben to a national and international audience, making him a relatable figure for many young people aspiring to follow practical trades or start their own businesses. His candidness, work ethic, and down-to-earth nature resonated with viewers, earning him respect and admiration.

2. Social Media and Online Following

Beyond traditional media, Reuben has built a presence on social media platforms where he shares insights into his work, daily life, and projects. His authentic approach free from glamour or pretense has attracted a following interested in rural life, machinery, and entrepreneurship. This digital engagement allows him to connect directly with fans, inspire aspiring tradespeople, and promote the value of hands-on skills.

3. Role Model for Youth and Tradespeople

Reuben's public image is that of a young man who embraces hard work and self-reliance, making him a positive role model for youth, especially those who may feel uncertain about non-academic career paths. By demonstrating success through practical skills and determination, he challenges stereotypes and promotes respect for skilled trades.

Educational programs and career advisors have noted his example as encouraging young people to consider vocational training and entrepreneurship, areas often overlooked in traditional career guidance.

4. Recognition Within the Rural and Agricultural Communities

Locally, Reuben is well respected as a capable tradesman and reliable worker. His reputation for professionalism and quality workmanship has earned him recognition in the rural communities of the Yorkshire Dales and beyond. This peer recognition is critical in an industry built largely on trust and word-of-mouth.

5. Inspiring Future Generations

By openly sharing his journey including both successes and setbacks Reuben has become a source of inspiration for those who wish to carve out their own path in the trades, farming, or rural businesses. His story encourages others to value practical education, persistence, and passion.

Reuben Owen's public recognition is multi-faceted, combining media visibility, social influence, and genuine respect from both peers and the wider public. His evolving role as a young entrepreneur and role model continues to grow, reflecting the power of authenticity and hard work in today's world.

CHAPTER 5

Personal Life

Family and Relationships

Reuben Owen's life and career are deeply intertwined with his family, whose influence and support have been pivotal throughout his journey. The values, relationships, and experiences within his family environment have shaped both his personal character and professional ambitions.

1. The Owen Family Foundation

Reuben was born into the Owen family, custodians of Ravenseat Farm a remote and rugged hill farm located in the Yorkshire Dales, England. The farm has been in the family for generations, embodying a legacy of hard work, resilience, and connection to the land. His parents, Clive and Emma Owen, have been central figures in his life, not only providing a strong familial foundation but also modeling dedication, perseverance, and practical skills.

Growing up in this environment, Reuben absorbed the importance of family cooperation, self-sufficiency, and respect for tradition values that continue to influence his work ethic and personal life.

2. Relationship with Parents

Clive Owen, Reuben's father, is a key mentor and supporter. Their relationship is characterized by mutual respect, shared passion for the land, and collaboration on both farm and business ventures. Clive's experience and guidance have helped Reuben navigate the challenges of rural entrepreneurship, offering advice, encouragement, and hands-on assistance when needed.

Emma Owen, his mother, has also played a nurturing and stabilizing role in Reuben's life, balancing the demands of farm life with the emotional and practical needs of her children. Her support has been integral to maintaining family cohesion amid the pressures of public life.

3. Sibling Bonds

Reuben shares a close bond with his siblings, who also feature prominently in the family's story as documented in television series. These relationships provide a sense of camaraderie and shared purpose. The siblings often collaborate on farm tasks, support each other's endeavors, and maintain a strong family network despite the demanding nature of their lifestyle.

4. Friendships and Community Ties

Beyond immediate family, Reuben values friendships and relationships within the local community. Living and working in a rural area fosters close connections with neighbors, fellow farmers, and clients. These relationships are based on trust, mutual respect, and a shared understanding of the challenges and rewards of rural life.

Reuben's reputation for reliability and integrity has helped him build a solid network of professional and personal contacts, contributing to both his social support system and business opportunities.

5. Personal Life and Future Aspirations

While Reuben maintains a degree of privacy around his personal romantic relationships, it is clear that family remains at the core of his life. His aspirations include not only expanding his business but also preserving the family farm's heritage and contributing to the community that has supported him.

He often speaks about the importance of balance between work and family, tradition and innovation as he looks toward the future.

Reuben Owen's family and relationships form the bedrock of his life story. The close-knit support system, combined with a strong sense of duty and connection to his roots, continues to inspire his growth both personally and professionally.

Hobbies and Interests

Beyond his professional life and family commitments, Reuben Owen has cultivated a range of hobbies and interests that reflect his personality, values, and connection to the rural environment in which he was raised. These activities offer insight into the young man behind the public figure and provide balance to his busy and demanding schcdule.

1. Love for Machinery and Mechanical Work

From a young age, Reuben showed a strong fascination with machinery, engines, and mechanical systems. This interest goes beyond his business; he enjoys working on and maintaining his own diggers, tractors, and farm equipment. Whether it's repairing a hydraulic system or fine-tuning an engine, Reuben finds satisfaction in understanding how things work and ensuring that machines run smoothly.

This hobby aligns perfectly with his professional career, allowing him to deepen his expertise and remain hands-on with the tools of his trade.

2. Outdoor Activities and Nature Appreciation

Growing up in the Yorkshire Dales has fostered a profound appreciation for nature and the outdoors. Reuben enjoys spending time outside, whether it's hiking across the hills, fishing in local streams, or simply exploring the countryside. These activities provide relaxation and a way to connect with the landscape that forms the backdrop of his life and work.

His respect for the environment also influences his approach to farming and groundwork, emphasizing sustainable practices and conservation.

3. Farming and Animal Care

While his primary focus has shifted toward machinery and groundwork, Reuben remains actively involved in the farming lifestyle. He participates in animal care and farm maintenance, activities that require patience, responsibility, and practical skills. This connection to farming roots keeps him grounded and connected to his family's heritage.

4. Interest in Rural Crafts and Traditional Skills

Reuben has shown an interest in rural crafts such as stone wall building, fencing, and woodworking. These skills, often passed down through generations, complement his mechanical abilities and contribute to the preservation of rural traditions. Engaging in these crafts allows him to blend the old with the new, respecting the past while embracing modern techniques.

5. Media and Storytelling

With his involvement in television, Reuben has also developed an appreciation for storytelling and media production. He understands the power of sharing authentic stories about rural life and trades, and occasionally participates in interviews and filming with enthusiasm. This interest may open doors to further opportunities in media or advocacy related to rural communities and trades.

Reuben Owen's hobbies and interests reflect a well-rounded individual with a deep connection to his environment, a passion for practical skills, and a desire to balance work with recreation. These interests enrich his life and complement his professional endeavors, shaping him into the person admired by many.

Personal Values and Beliefs

Reuben Owen's character and decisions are deeply rooted in a set of personal values and beliefs shaped by his upbringing, experiences, and the rural community around him. These guiding principles have influenced his approach to life, work, and relationships, underpinning his integrity and authenticity.

1. Hard Work and Determination

A cornerstone of Reuben's ethos is a strong belief in the value of hard work. Raised on a family farm where long days and physical labor are the norm, he embraces the idea that success is earned through perseverance, effort, and dedication. This value drives his commitment to his groundwork business and his continual learning and improvement.

He often expresses pride in accomplishing tasks with his own hands, seeing effort not as a burden but as a pathway to growth and fulfillment.

2. Honesty and Integrity

Reuben places great importance on honesty and integrity in both personal and professional dealings. Trustworthiness is essential in rural communities where reputation is built on word-of-mouth and long-term relationships. He strives to be reliable, transparent, and fair, ensuring that clients, colleagues, and family can depend on him.

This commitment to integrity has been fundamental to building his business and earning respect within his community.

3. Respect for Tradition and Family

Despite his entrepreneurial ambitions, Reuben holds a deep respect for tradition and family heritage. Growing up on Ravenseat Farm instilled in him an appreciation for the legacy passed down through generations and the importance of preserving this history.

He values the lessons learned from older family members and the wisdom embedded in rural customs, seeing them as a foundation upon which to build the future.

4. Connection to Nature and Sustainability

Living in the Yorkshire Dales has fostered a strong connection to nature and an awareness of environmental stewardship. Reuben believes in working with the land rather than against it, embracing sustainable practices in farming and groundwork to protect the natural environment for future generations.

This respect for the outdoors influences his decisions and inspires a thoughtful approach to resource use and conservation.

5. Independence and Self-Reliance

A key belief that motivates Reuben is the value of independence and taking responsibility for one's own path. His journey into business ownership reflects a desire to be self-reliant, make his own decisions, and carve out a unique identity apart from family legacy.

He encourages others, especially young people, to develop practical skills and confidence in their abilities as a means to achieve personal freedom and success.

Reuben Owen's personal values and beliefs reveal a young man grounded in tradition yet forward-looking, committed to honesty, hard work, and sustainability. These principles shape his approach to life and work, earning him respect and serving as a guide for his future endeavors.

CHAPTER 6

Impact and Legacy

Contributions to Society or Industry

Though still early in his career, Reuben Owen has made notable contributions to both his local community and the broader groundwork and rural trades industry. His work, public presence, and approach to business demonstrate a commitment to making a positive impact that extends beyond his personal success.

1. Promoting Skilled Trades and Rural Entrepreneurship

One of Reuben's most significant contributions is his role in raising awareness and respect for skilled trades and rural entrepreneurship. Through his television appearances and social media presence, he has highlighted the opportunities and rewards that come with working in practical, hands-on professions. This challenges societal perceptions that prioritize academic or office-based careers, inspiring young people to consider alternative, valuable paths.

By showcasing the real-life challenges and triumphs of starting and running a groundwork business, Reuben helps demystify rural trades and encourages economic development in less urbanized areas.

2. Supporting Sustainable Practices in Groundwork and Farming

Reuben's respect for the environment translates into practical contributions toward sustainable land management and farming practices. Through careful planning and execution of groundwork projects, he emphasizes minimizing environmental impact, protecting soil integrity, and maintaining natural habitats.

His approach serves as a model for balancing business growth with ecological responsibility, contributing to the sustainability of rural landscapes and farming communities.

3. Strengthening Local Economies

By operating a local business and contracting with farmers, homeowners, and small enterprises, Reuben plays a role in supporting the rural economy. His work helps maintain and improve vital infrastructure, enabling agricultural productivity and enhancing the quality of life in his community.

Moreover, his business creates opportunities for other local suppliers and tradespeople, fostering a network of mutual support and economic resilience.

4. Inspiring Youth and Community Engagement

Reuben's visibility as a young entrepreneur and skilled tradesman serves as a source of inspiration for youth, particularly in rural areas where employment options may be limited. By sharing his journey openly, including challenges faced and lessons learned, he encourages others to pursue their goals with determination and integrity.

This influence extends to community engagement, where Reuben is seen as a positive role model who values tradition while embracing innovation.

5. Contribution to Media Representation of Rural Life

Through Beyond the Yorkshire Farm and related media projects, Reuben contributes to a more authentic representation of rural life and work. These portrayals help bridge the gap between urban audiences and the realities of farming and trades, fostering greater appreciation and understanding.

By humanizing rural entrepreneurship and highlighting the skills involved, he elevates the status of countryside professions in popular culture.

Reuben Owen's contributions to society and industry are multifaceted, spanning economic support, environmental stewardship, youth inspiration, and media representation. His ongoing efforts reflect a commitment to building a sustainable, respected, and vibrant rural trades sector.

Influence on Others

Reuben Owen's journey from a rural upbringing to becoming a recognized tradesman and young entrepreneur has had a meaningful influence on a wide range of people from family and friends to fans and aspiring tradespeople. His authenticity, work ethic, and openness have inspired many in different ways.

1. Inspiration to Young People and Aspiring Tradesmen

Reuben serves as a relatable role model for young people, particularly those considering non-traditional career paths. By openly sharing his experiences on television and social media, he encourages others to embrace vocational skills, hard work, and entrepreneurship. His story helps break down stigmas around trades as less desirable compared to academic careers, showing that success and fulfillment are achievable through practical work.

Many young viewers have expressed admiration for Reuben's determination and self-reliance, finding motivation to pursue apprenticeships, training, or start their own ventures.

2. Encouraging Rural Entrepreneurship

Reuben's example promotes the idea that rural areas can be hubs of innovation and economic activity. His ability to start and grow a groundwork business in a remote location demonstrates that entrepreneurship is not confined to cities. This has inspired other rural dwellers to explore business opportunities that leverage local resources and skills.

His influence supports efforts to revitalize rural economies and encourage sustainable development.

3. Positive Impact on Family and Community

Within his own family, Reuben is a source of support and inspiration, motivating siblings and relatives to pursue their goals with dedication. His role in the family business and farm operations strengthens familial bonds and sets a standard for responsibility and teamwork.

In the local community, his reputation for reliability and integrity influences others to uphold similar values. His interactions with clients and neighbors foster a spirit of cooperation and trust.

4. Changing Perceptions Through Media

Reuben's presence in popular media contributes to shifting public perceptions of rural life and skilled trades. By showcasing the challenges and rewards of groundwork and farm life in an honest and engaging way, he helps audiences appreciate the skill, resilience, and passion involved.

This influence extends to educational and vocational discussions, where his story is used to highlight the value of hands-on professions.

5. Mentorship and Guidance

Though still early in his career, Reuben has begun to informally mentor others interested in trades or rural business. Whether through social media interactions, community involvement, or direct advice, he offers practical guidance and encouragement to those following similar paths.

His willingness to share knowledge and experiences fosters a supportive network that benefits individuals and the wider trades community.

Reuben Owen's influence reaches far beyond his immediate environment. Through inspiration, example, and active engagement, he empowers others to value practical skills, pursue their ambitions, and contribute positively to their communities.

Awards and Honors

While Reuben Owen's career is still in its early stages, he has already received recognition that underscores his achievements and growing reputation as a skilled tradesman and young entrepreneur in the rural trades industry.

1. Recognition from Local and Industry Groups

Reuben's commitment to quality workmanship and professionalism has earned him praise and informal accolades from local agricultural and trade organizations. His dedication to sustainable and reliable groundwork practices has made him a respected figure in community forums and trade networks within the Yorkshire Dales and surrounding areas.

Though not always formal awards, this peer recognition is a meaningful testament to his standing within the rural trades community.

2. Media and Viewer Appreciation

The success of Beyond the Yorkshire Farm and the positive response from viewers can be considered a form of public honor. Reuben's ability to connect with audiences and represent rural entrepreneurship authentically has been celebrated by fans and media alike, contributing to his rising profile.

The show's acclaim and its role in increasing awareness of rural trades reflect well on Reuben's personal and professional image.

3. Potential Future Honors

As Reuben continues to build his business and expand his influence, there is strong potential for formal recognition. Industry awards for young entrepreneurs, rural business excellence, or skilled trades achievement could highlight his contributions in the years ahead.

His growing social media presence and media profile also position him well for honors related to community engagement and positive role modeling.

while formal awards for Reuben Owen may still be emerging, the respect and recognition he has gained from his community, peers, and media audiences are significant milestones. These honors underscore his impact and promise in the trades and rural entrepreneurship sectors.

CHAPTER 7

Challenges and Controversies
Public Criticisms

As with many public figures, especially those featured in media and popular television, Reuben Owen has faced some public criticisms and challenges alongside his successes. These critiques provide insight into the pressures and expectations that come with visibility, as well as the complexity of balancing personal and professional life in the public eye.

1. Perceptions of Privilege

One common criticism has been related to the perception that Reuben benefits from his family's established farm business and media exposure. Some viewers and commentators argue that his opportunities and initial platform have been influenced significantly by his family's reputation and resources, rather than solely his individual merit.

While this critique highlights debates about privilege and access, Reuben has consistently worked to prove his own skills, dedication, and entrepreneurial spirit beyond the family name.

2. Reality vs. Television

As with many reality-based or documentary-style TV programs, some critics question the authenticity or completeness of the portrayal of Reuben's life and work. There are occasional discussions about the extent to which the shows capture the full scope of challenges, the day-to-day grind, or the financial pressures involved.

Reuben and his family have acknowledged the role of editing and production in shaping narratives, emphasizing that while not every moment is shown, the core stories remain true to their experiences.

3. Public Scrutiny and Privacy

Increased media attention inevitably brings scrutiny of personal decisions, lifestyle choices, and family matters. Some critics feel that the show sometimes exposes more of their private lives than desired, leading to discussions about boundaries between public and private spheres.

Reuben has expressed the importance of maintaining a balance, valuing transparency but also protecting the well-being of family members.

4. Business Challenges Highlighted Publicly

Some critics have noted that the public airing of business challenges or setbacks could impact perceptions of professionalism or reliability. While transparency about struggles can foster empathy and realism, it can also invite judgment or doubts from potential clients or partners.

Reuben has handled such situations by focusing on resilience and learning, viewing challenges as part of growth rather than failure.

while Reuben Owen has faced public criticisms typical for a media-exposed figure, these challenges have also highlighted his resilience and commitment to authenticity. He continues to navigate the complexities of public life with openness and a focus on personal and professional integrity.

How He Overcame Obstacles

Reuben Owen's journey, like that of many entrepreneurs and public figures, has not been without its challenges. His ability to navigate and overcome obstacles has been a key factor in his growth, both personally and professionally. These experiences reveal his resilience, adaptability, and determination.

1. Facing Skepticism and Proving His Worth

Early in his career, Reuben faced skepticism from some quarters who questioned whether his success was due to family connections or media exposure rather than his own skills. Instead of being discouraged, he used this criticism as motivation to demonstrate his capabilities. Through consistent hard work, learning on the job, and delivering quality workmanship, he built a reputation based on merit.

Reuben's focus on competence and reliability gradually silenced doubts and earned him respect within the trades community.

2. Managing Business Pressures and Financial Challenges

Running a small groundwork business in a rural area comes with financial and operational hurdles, such as fluctuating demand, equipment costs, and competition. Reuben confronted these realities by careful planning, maintaining a lean operation, and continuously improving his skills in machinery and business management.

When setbacks occurred, he treated them as learning opportunities rather than failures, which helped him refine his strategies and grow stronger.

3. Balancing Public Life and Privacy

Becoming a television personality brought both opportunity and scrutiny. Reuben had to learn how to balance the demands of public attention with his desire for a private personal life. This required setting boundaries, communicating clearly with media teams, and protecting his family's well-being.

By maintaining a grounded perspective and focusing on what mattered most, he managed to keep his personal values intact despite external pressures.

4. Physical and Mental Demands of the Work

Groundwork and farming are physically demanding and sometimes hazardous. Reuben's resilience has been tested by the strenuous nature of his work, harsh weather conditions, and long hours. He overcame these challenges by cultivating good health habits, using safety equipment, and developing a strong work ethic.

Mentally, he maintains focus by setting clear goals and drawing motivation from his passion for the craft and connection to the land.

5. Embracing Learning and Adaptation

Reuben recognizes that continual learning is essential to overcoming obstacles. Whether it's mastering new machinery, understanding business finance, or adapting to changing industry standards, he remains open to growth.

This willingness to learn, adapt, and innovate has enabled him to navigate uncertainties and position his business for future success.

Reuben Owen's approach to overcoming obstacles combines resilience, hard work, strategic thinking, and a commitment to personal values. These qualities have helped him face challenges head-on and emerge stronger, paving the way for continued progress.

CHAPTER 8

Current Life and Future Plans

Recent Activities

In the past few years, Reuben Owen has been actively building on his early successes, both in his groundwork business and as a public figure.

Business Expansion: Reuben has taken on larger and more diverse groundwork projects around the Yorkshire Dales, investing in better equipment and expanding his team. This growth reflects his commitment to establishing a sustainable and respected local enterprise.

Media Engagement: He continues to feature in Beyond the Yorkshire Farm and maintains an active presence on social media platforms, sharing insights into his daily work, machinery operation, and rural life. His online content has helped inspire a broader audience interested in skilled trades and farming.

Community Involvement: Reuben participates in local events and supports initiatives aimed at promoting vocational skills and rural entrepreneurship among young people in his community.

Skills Development: He remains focused on personal growth through training in areas like machinery safety, business management, and sustainable farming techniques, ensuring his work meets evolving industry standards.

Sustainable Practices: Recently, Reuben has shown increased interest in adopting environmentally friendly methods in both his groundwork projects and farming activities, aligning his business with broader sustainability goals.

Vision for the Future

Reuben Owen's vision for the future is shaped by his passion for rural trades, commitment to sustainability, and desire to inspire others. As he looks ahead, his goals reflect both personal ambition and a broader dedication to community and industry development.

1. Growing a Sustainable and Innovative Business

Reuben aims to expand his groundwork and contracting business while embracing new technologies and sustainable practices. He envisions integrating eco-friendly machinery and techniques that reduce environmental impact, setting a standard for responsible rural entrepreneurship.

By growing his business sustainably, he hopes to create more local jobs and contribute positively to the Yorkshire Dales economy.

2. Championing Skilled Trades and Apprenticeships

Understanding the importance of skilled labor, Reuben plans to actively promote apprenticeships and training programs for young people interested in trades. He hopes to establish mentorship opportunities that provide hands-on experience and guidance, helping to address skill shortages and empower the next generation.

3. Expanding Media and Educational Outreach

Building on his media presence, Reuben envisions using platforms like television, social media, and community events to raise awareness about rural industries, practical skills, and entrepreneurship. He aims to provide authentic, educational content that inspires viewers to value and explore careers in trades.

4. Enhancing Community Impact

Reuben is committed to deepening his involvement in local initiatives that support rural development, environmental conservation, and youth engagement. He hopes to partner with organizations focused on improving infrastructure and economic opportunities in countryside areas.

5. Personal Growth and Lifelong Learning

Recognizing that growth is continuous, Reuben plans to pursue further education and training in areas such as business management, sustainable agriculture, and innovative construction methods. This ongoing learning will enable him to adapt to changing industry demands and lead with confidence.

Reuben Owen's vision for the future blends ambition with responsibility. He aims to be a leader in sustainable rural business, an advocate for skilled trades, and a positive influence in his community, ensuring his work benefits not only himself but the generations to come.

Conclusion

Summary of Key Points

Background: Reuben Owen hails from the Yorkshire Dales, where his family runs a farm and groundwork business, providing him with a strong connection to rural life and skilled trades from an early age.

Early Life and Education: Growing up immersed in farming and machinery, Reuben developed practical skills and a passion for groundwork and entrepreneurship.

Career Beginnings: He started working in the family business, quickly gaining hands-on experience in groundwork and contracting, building his reputation through hard work and reliability.

Breakthrough and Media Presence: Reuben gained wider recognition through his appearances on Beyond the Yorkshire Farm, which showcased his skills, work ethic, and rural lifestyle to a broad audience.

Business Growth: He has expanded his groundwork business, taking on more complex projects, investing in equipment, and emphasizing sustainable and environmentally responsible practices.

Community and Industry Contributions: Reuben actively supports rural development, apprenticeships, and vocational training, encouraging youth involvement in skilled trades and entrepreneurship.

Challenges and Resilience: He has overcome skepticism, financial and operational pressures, and public scrutiny by staying dedicated, adaptable, and committed to continuous learning.

Public Influence: Through media and personal example, Reuben inspires young people, promotes rural entrepreneurship, and contributes to a more positive perception of trades and countryside life.

Future Vision: Reuben aims to grow his business sustainably, expand mentorship programs, enhance media outreach, and deepen his community impact, all while continuing his personal and professional development.

Final Thoughts on Reuben Owen's Life

Reuben Owen's story is one of determination, resilience, and authentic passion for rural life and skilled trades. Emerging from the scenic yet challenging environment of the Yorkshire Dales, he has forged a path that honors both tradition and innovation. Through hard work, a commitment to learning, and a desire to uplift his community, Reuben exemplifies how dedication to one's craft can lead to personal success and broader social impact.

His journey highlights the value of trades as meaningful and rewarding careers, inspiring a new generation to consider alternatives to conventional academic routes. Despite public scrutiny and the pressures of media attention, Reuben has remained grounded in his values showing that integrity and perseverance are key to overcoming obstacles.

Looking ahead, Reuben's vision for sustainable business growth, community involvement, and skill development positions him as a promising figure in rural entrepreneurship. His life serves as a reminder that with passion and purpose, it is possible to build a fulfilling career while contributing positively to society and the environment.

Ultimately, Reuben Owen stands as a role model not just for aspiring tradespeople but for anyone seeking to balance ambition with authenticity in the modern world.

Printed in Dunstable, United Kingdom